THE BIRTH OF EARTH!
FUN FACTS ABOUT THE FORCES THAT SHAPED PLANET EARTH

Earth Science for Kids

Children's Earth Sciences Books

PRODIGYWIZARD
BOOKS

MY PLANET, OUR EARTH!

Hello, Earth! How were you formed? My natural curiosity asks me about your origin. Can you tell me about it?

Our planet Earth is the third planet from the Sun. Our planet is the largest among the terrestrial planets.

Amazingly, it is the only planet in our solar system that sustains life, as far as we know. It is the only planet that is not named after a deity.

Did you know that our planet was once like a world of lava?

The planet can have earthquakes, floods, and violent changes of temperature; but we can be thankful that today's Earth is calmer than before.

It took a long time to Earth to cool down from its hot, hot creation. The planet became temperate, in part because it developed an atmosphere.

Two-thirds of the planet is covered by water. Moderate temperatures, breathable atmosphere, and water provide excellent conditions for supporting life.

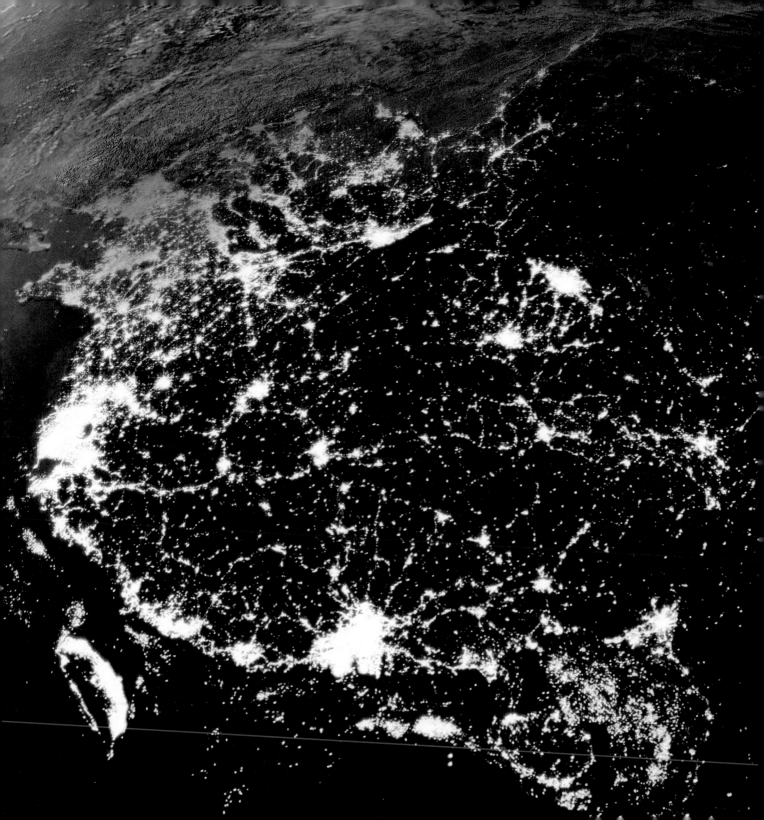

But, where did Earth come from? This is a very important question. Kids like you want to be informed of the origin of our planet.

At the start of the
Earth, there were
no human beings.
There was no one to
witness the Earth's
creation.

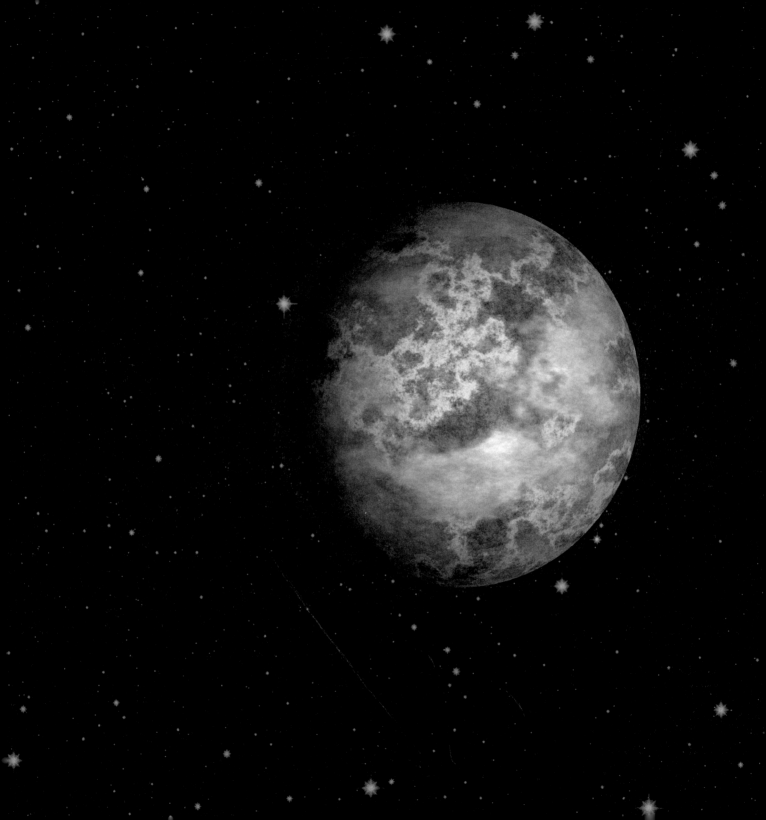

We count on our scientists, like the geographers who continuously conduct studies about our home planet.

They make their
educated theories
about how the
Earth came to be.
These hardworking
and patient people
give us facts and
help us understand
everything around us.

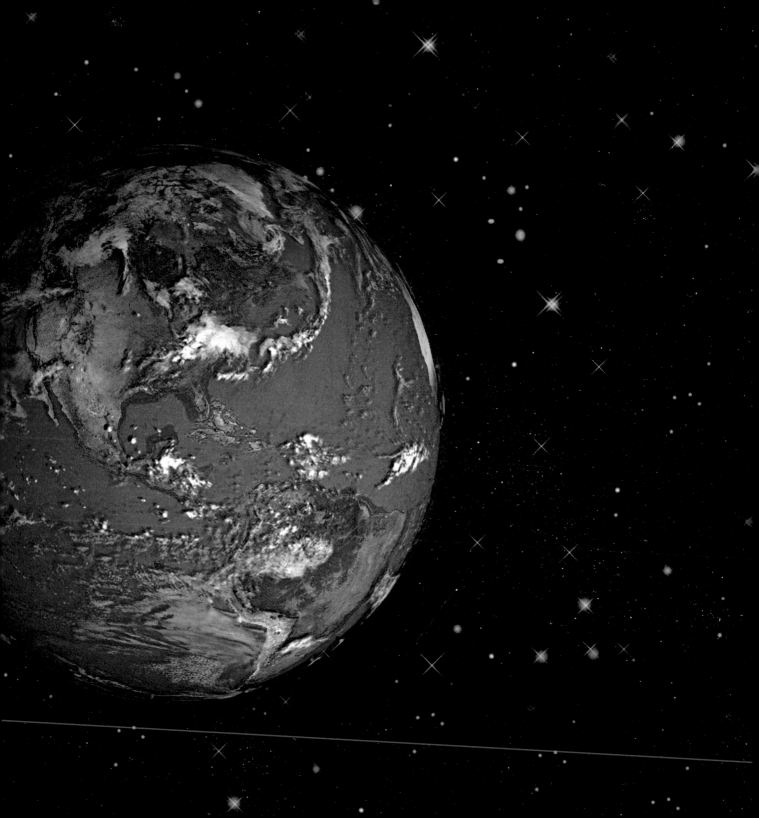

Along with the other planets, Earth came to be as a solidified cloud of dust and gases. The cloud was part of what was left over from the creation of the Sun.

According to the scientists, our solar system was nothing several billion years ago. Spinning through empty space was a cloud of cold dust particles.

The origin of Earth involves a solar nebula. It is a spinning cloud of dust. A nebula is a product of the Big Bang, the big explosion that created the universe.

The particles in the outer rings transformed into fiery balls. These large balls of gas and molten-liquid cooled and became solid. They became planets. One of them was Earth.

Roughly 4.48 billion years ago, the Earth's solar system was formed. The planet was relatively cool for about 500 million years.

Iron, silicates and small amounts of other elements are the main ingredients in the Earth's formation. Some of these elements are radioactive.

As millions of years passed, the Earth was heated by the energy released by radioactive decay. This process involved uranium, thorium and potassium.

The Earth's constituent elements began to melt. The iron and similar elements melted.

Thus, the Earth was born.
It took a long time to make
our home, the only planet
we know of that can
support life.

77693045R00024

Made in the USA
San Bernardino, CA
26 May 2018